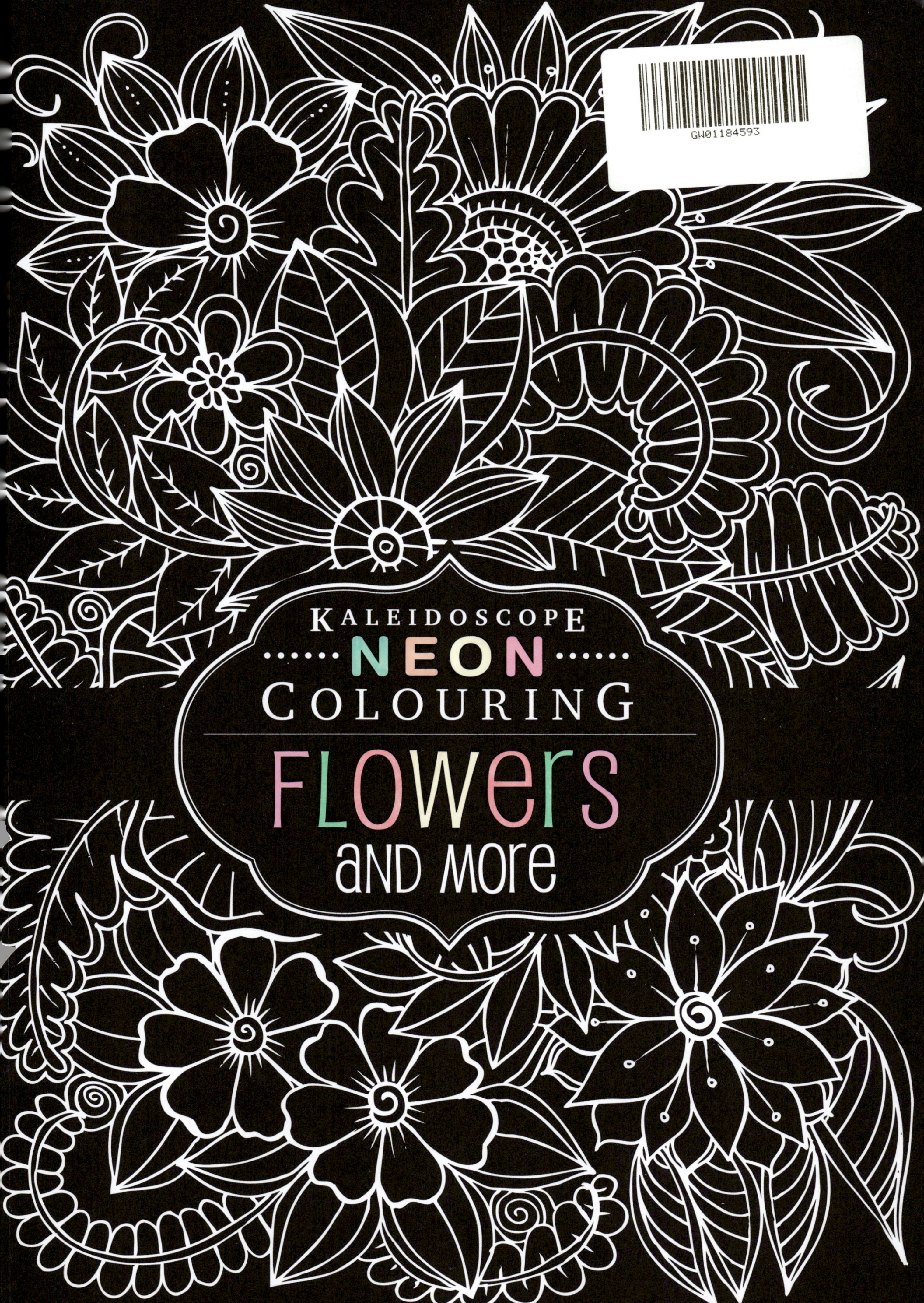

Kaleidoscope Neon Colouring

Flowers and More

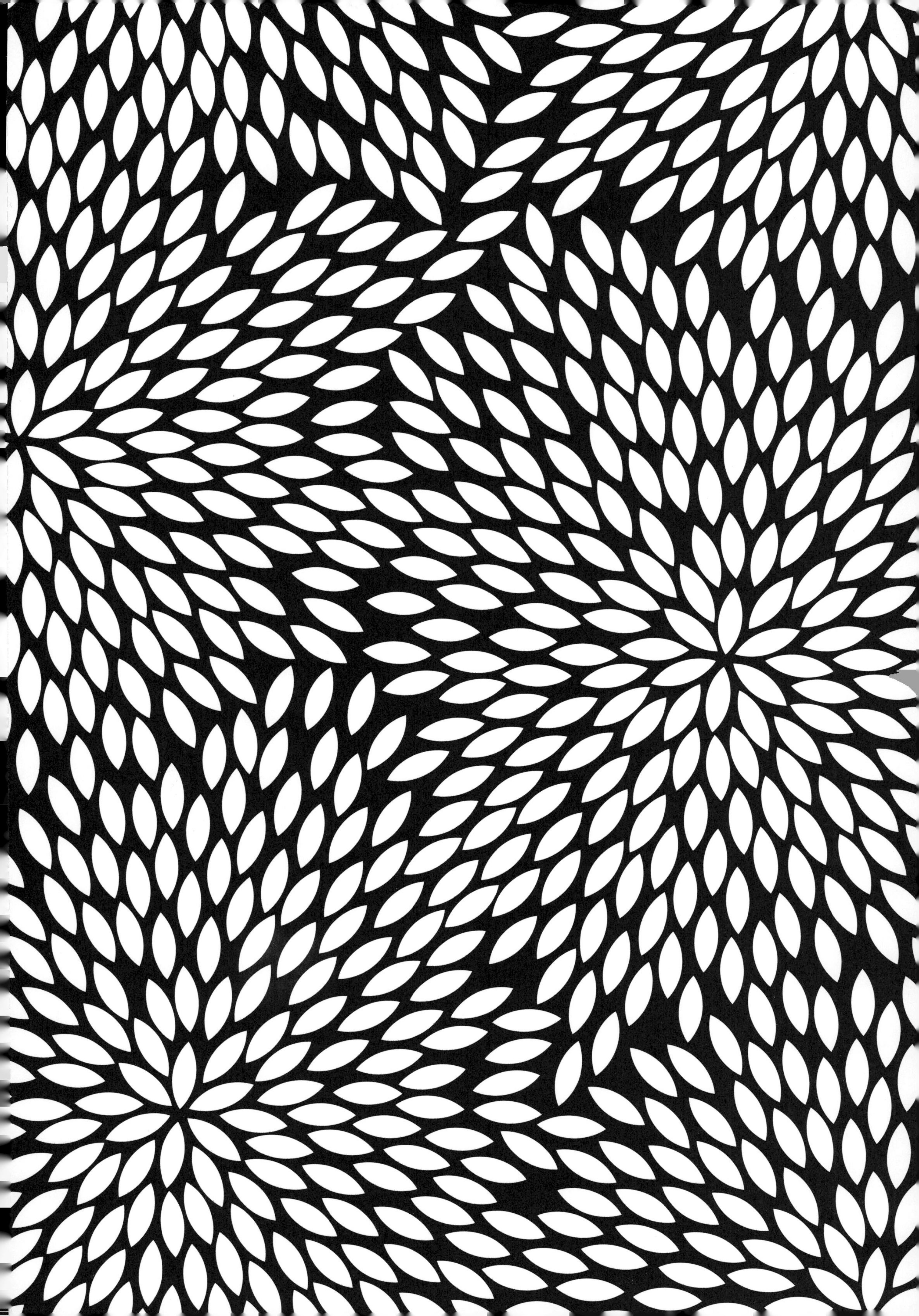

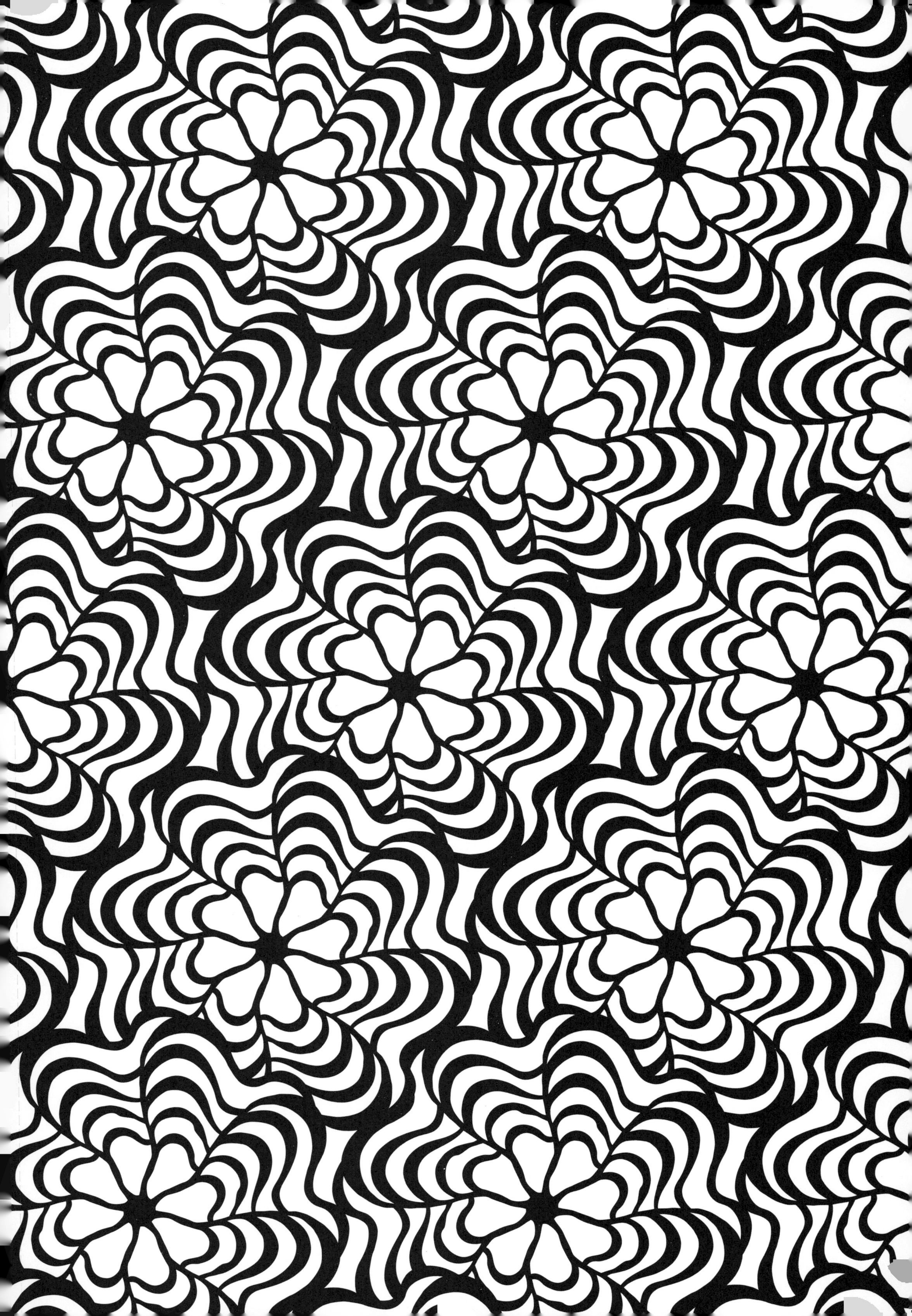

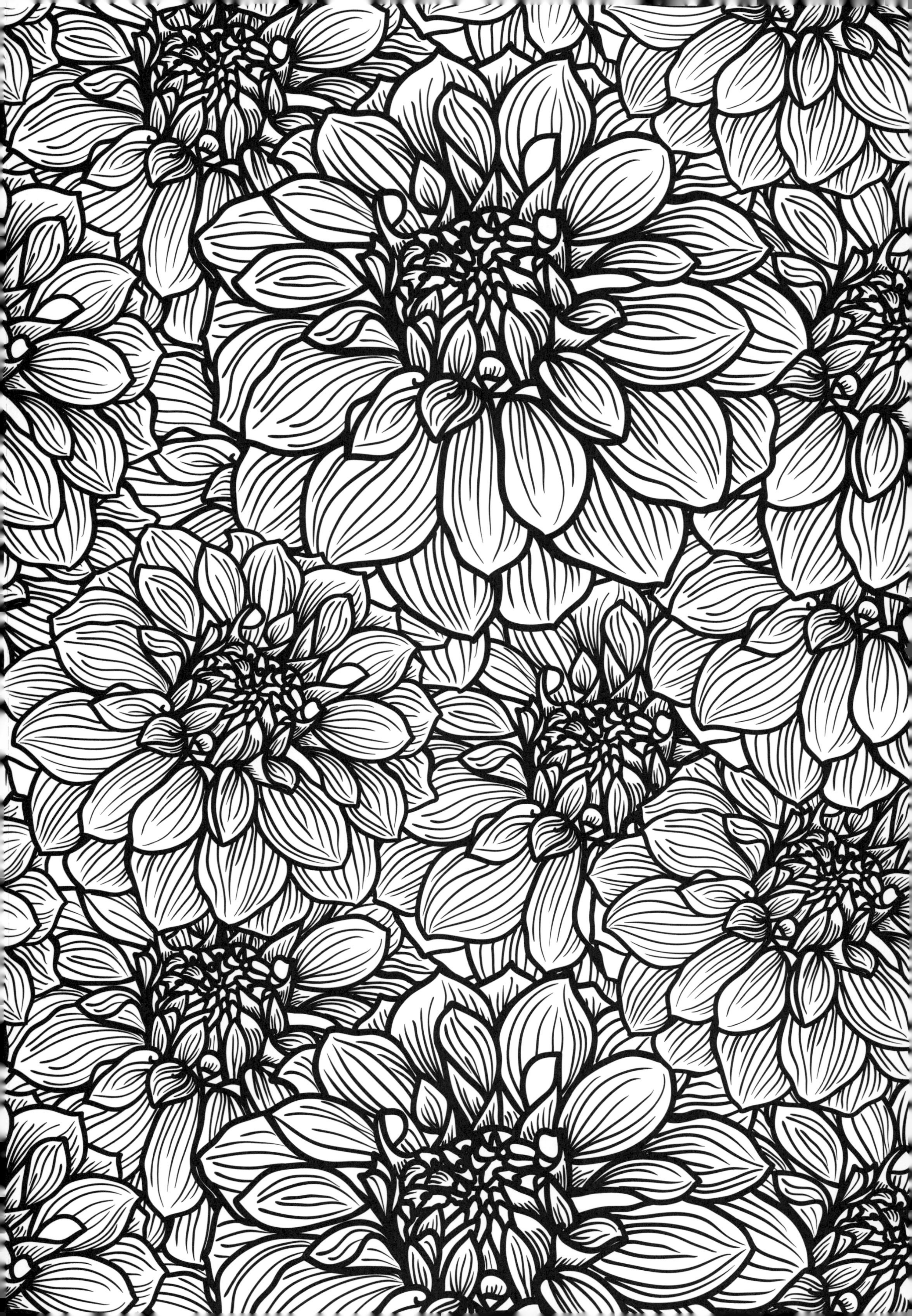

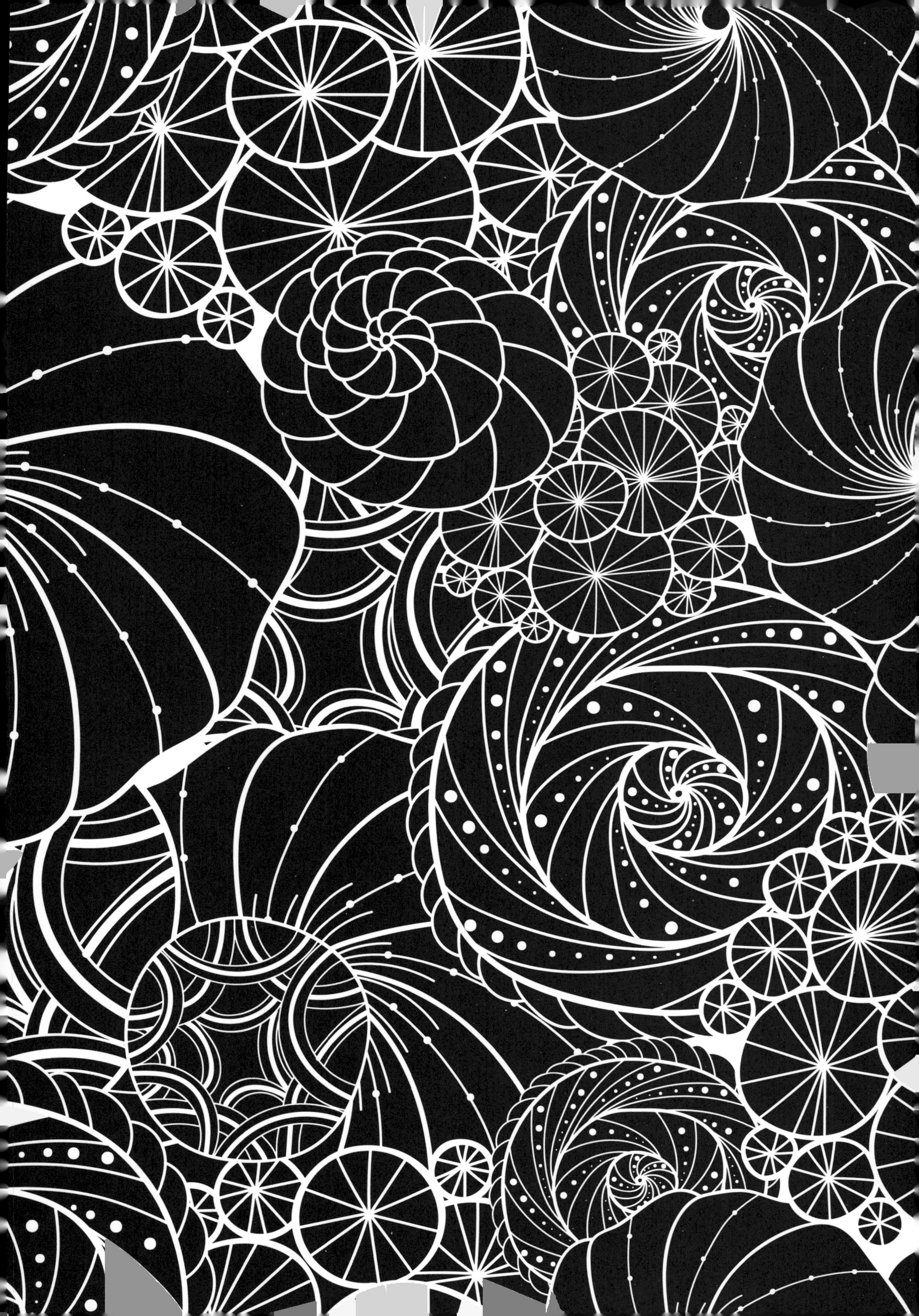

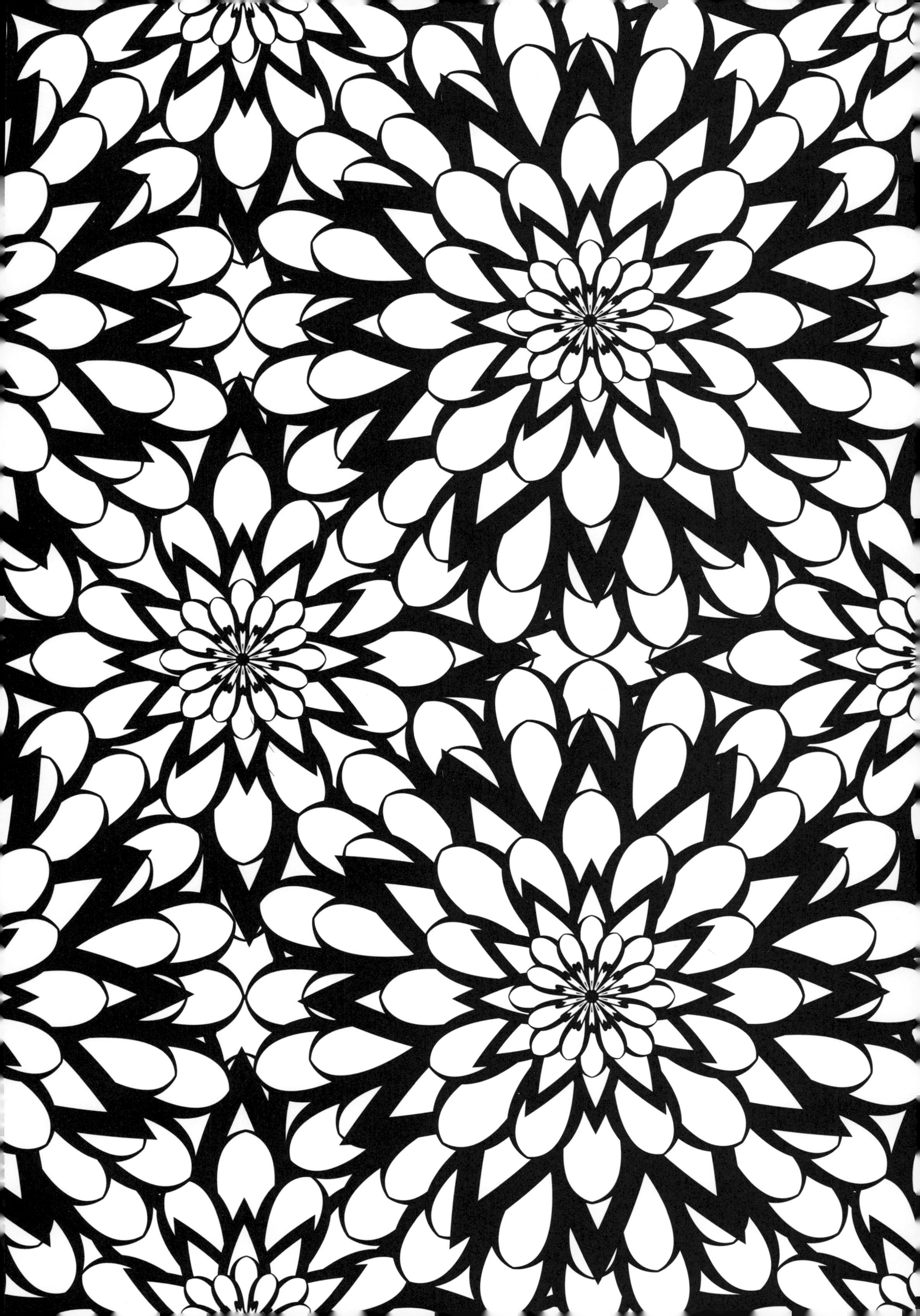

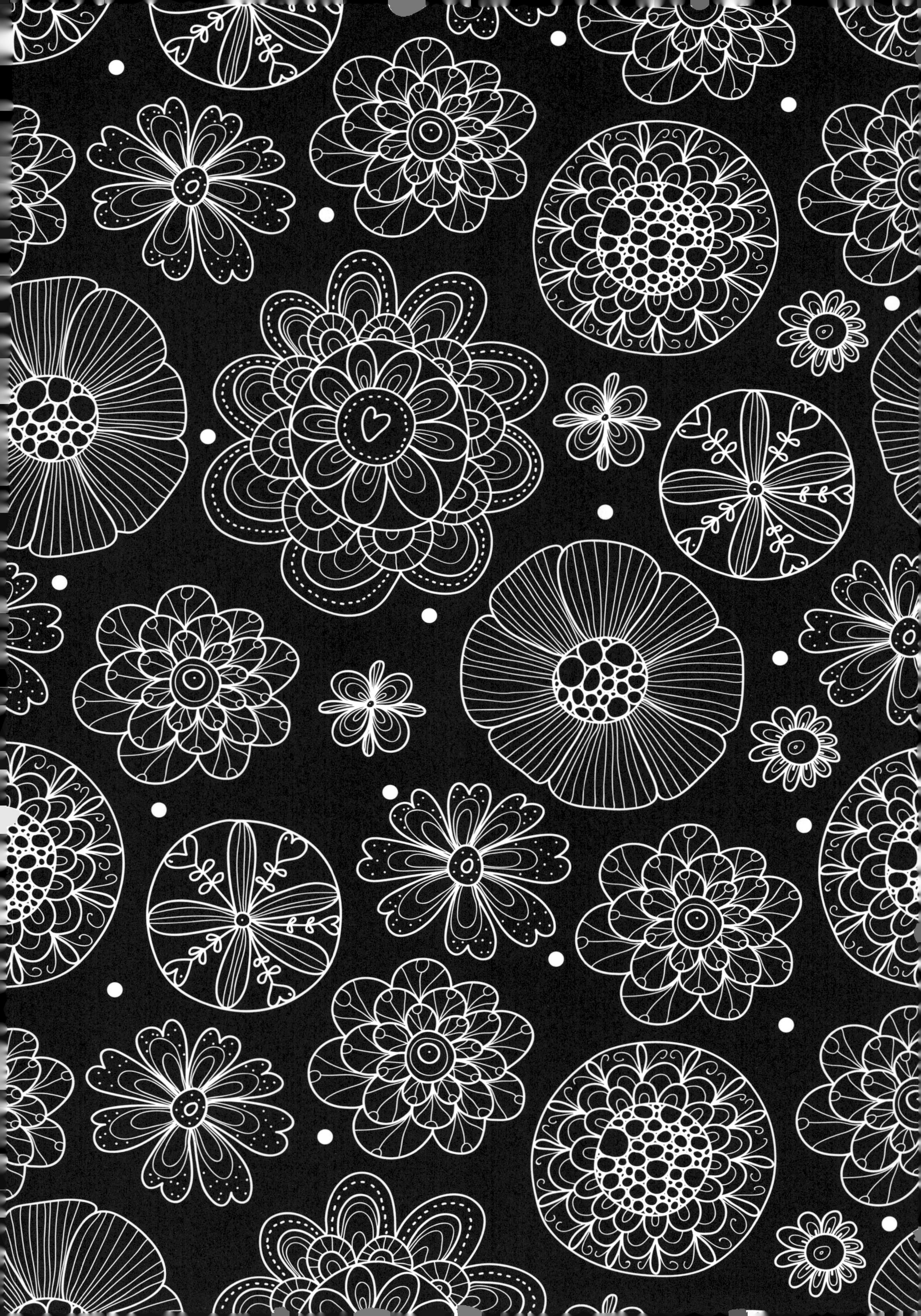

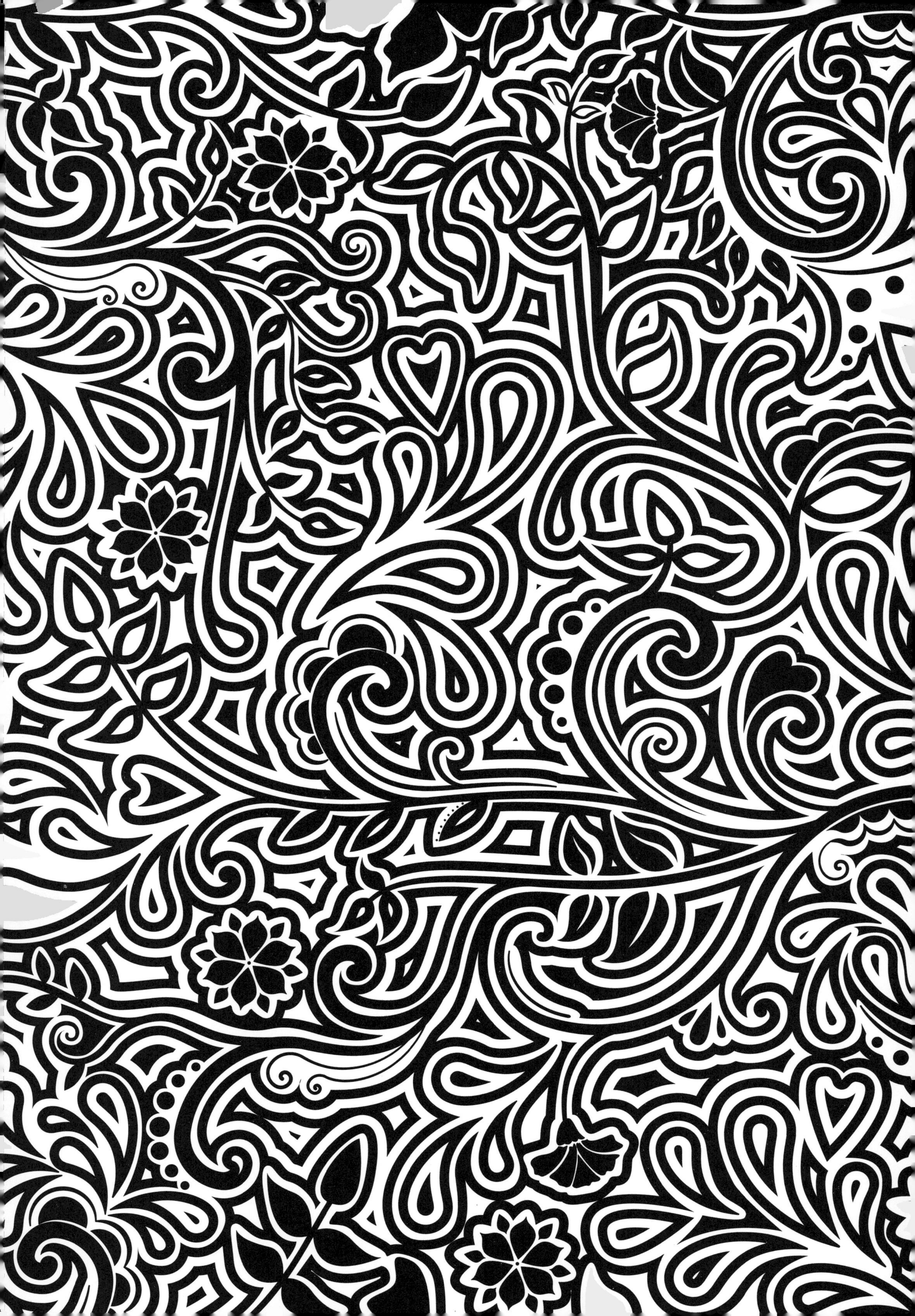

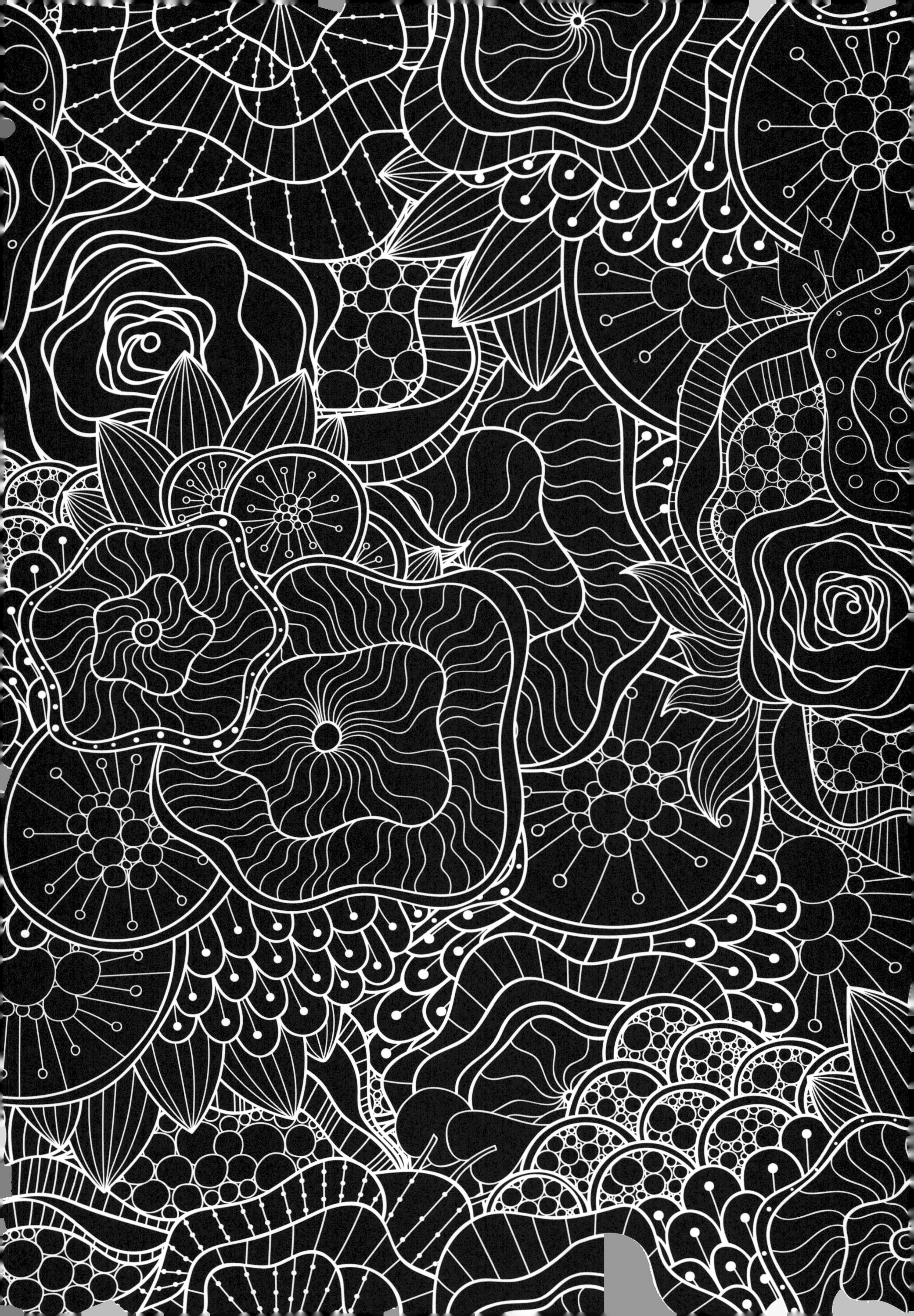

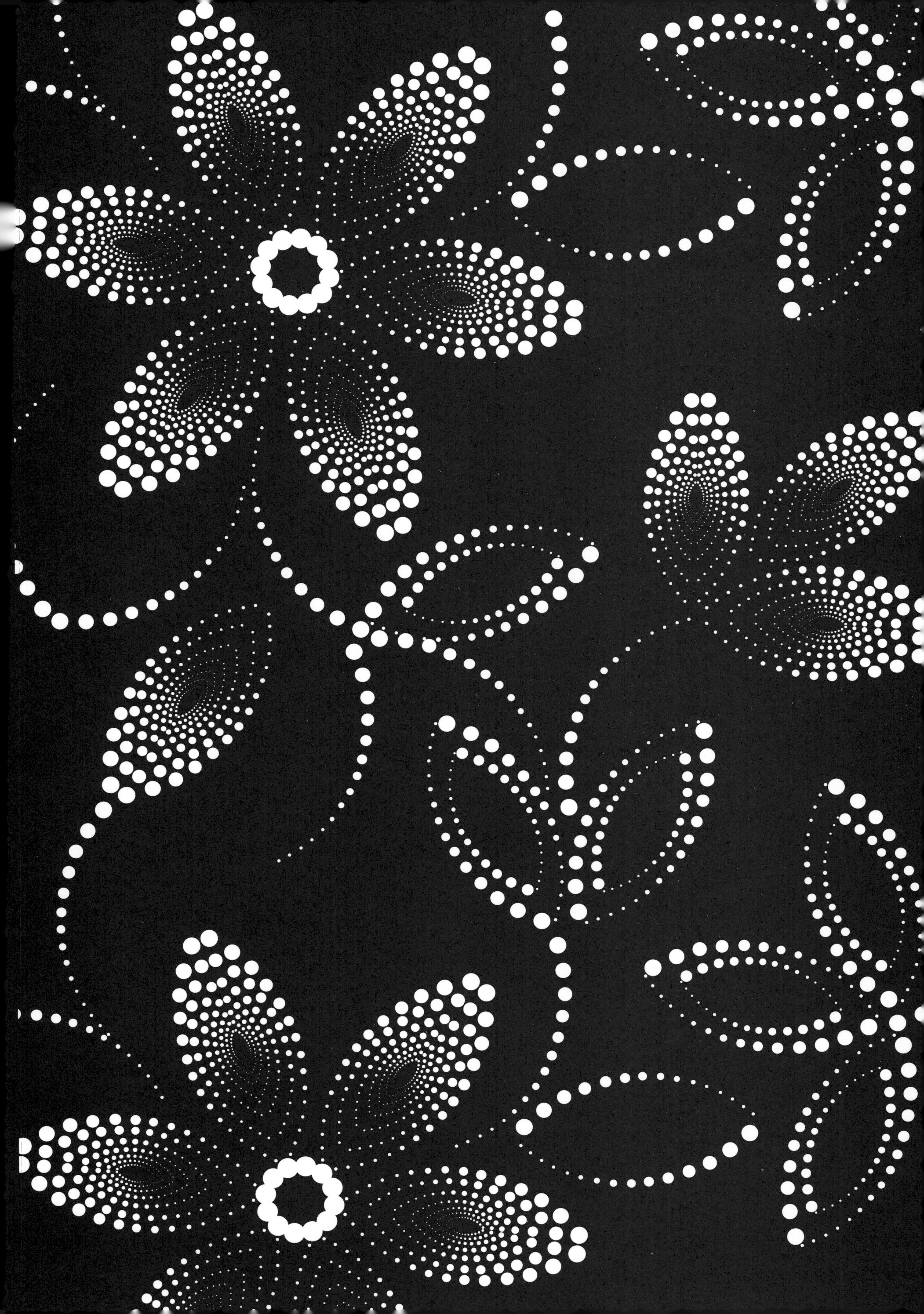

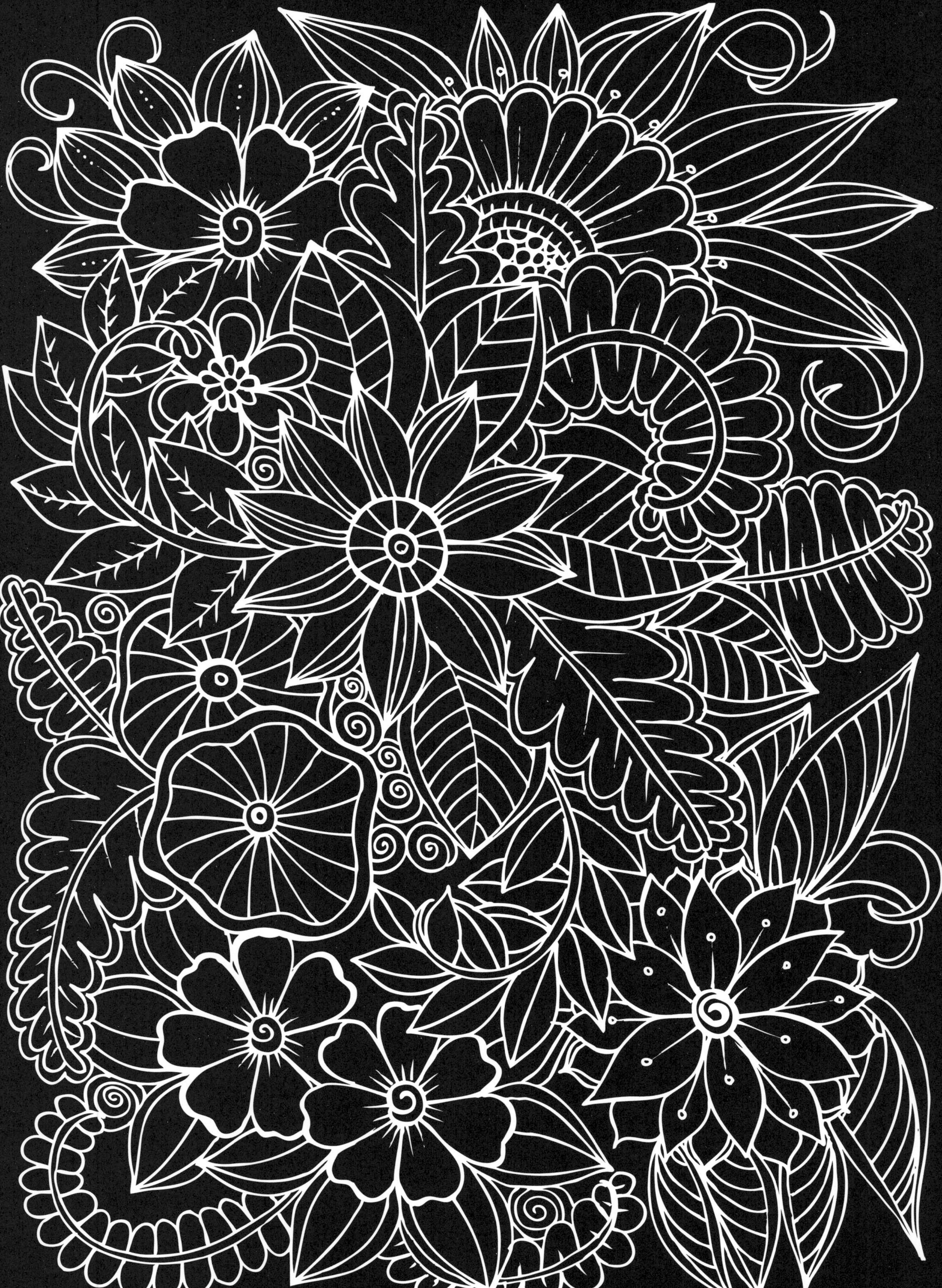

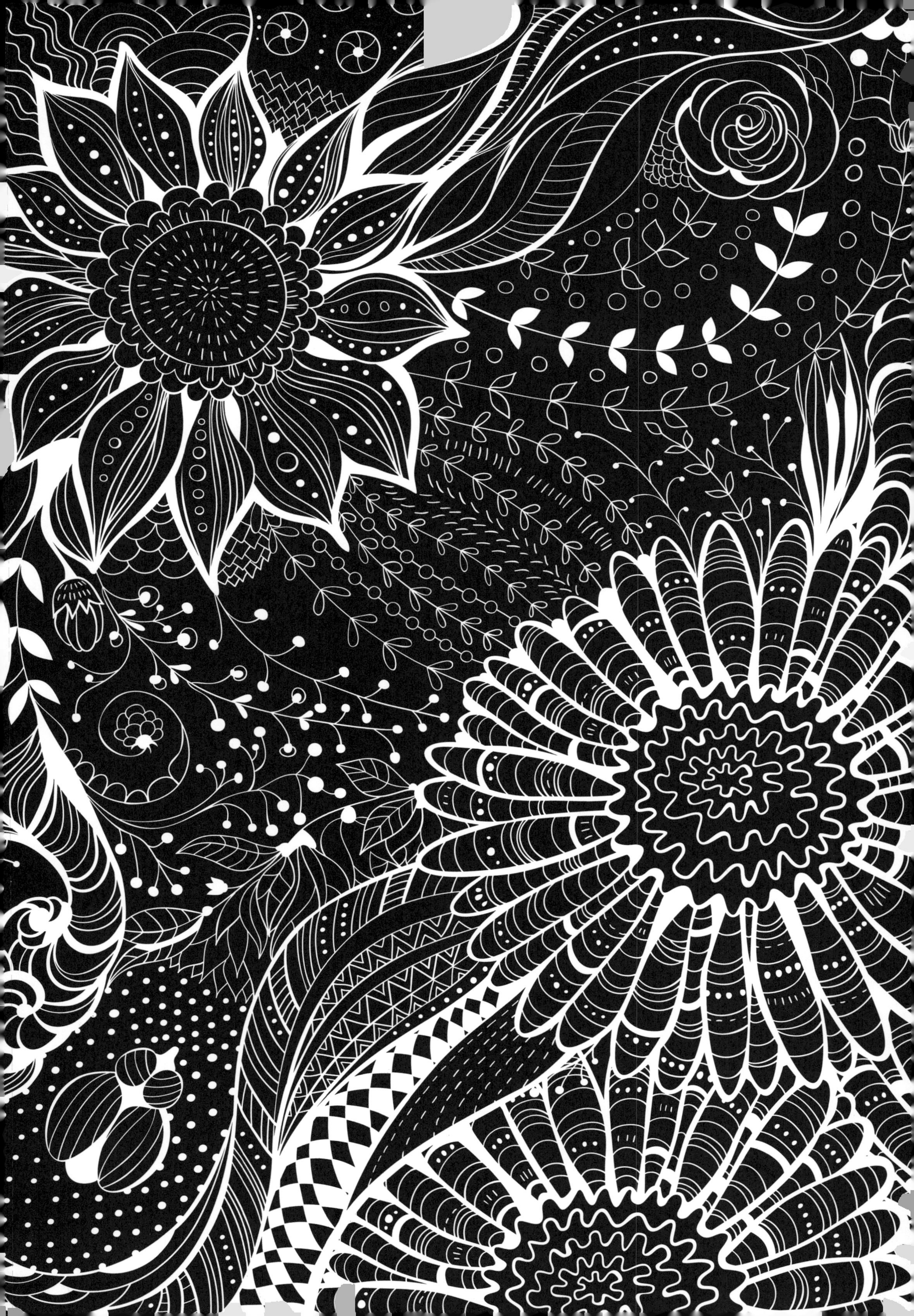

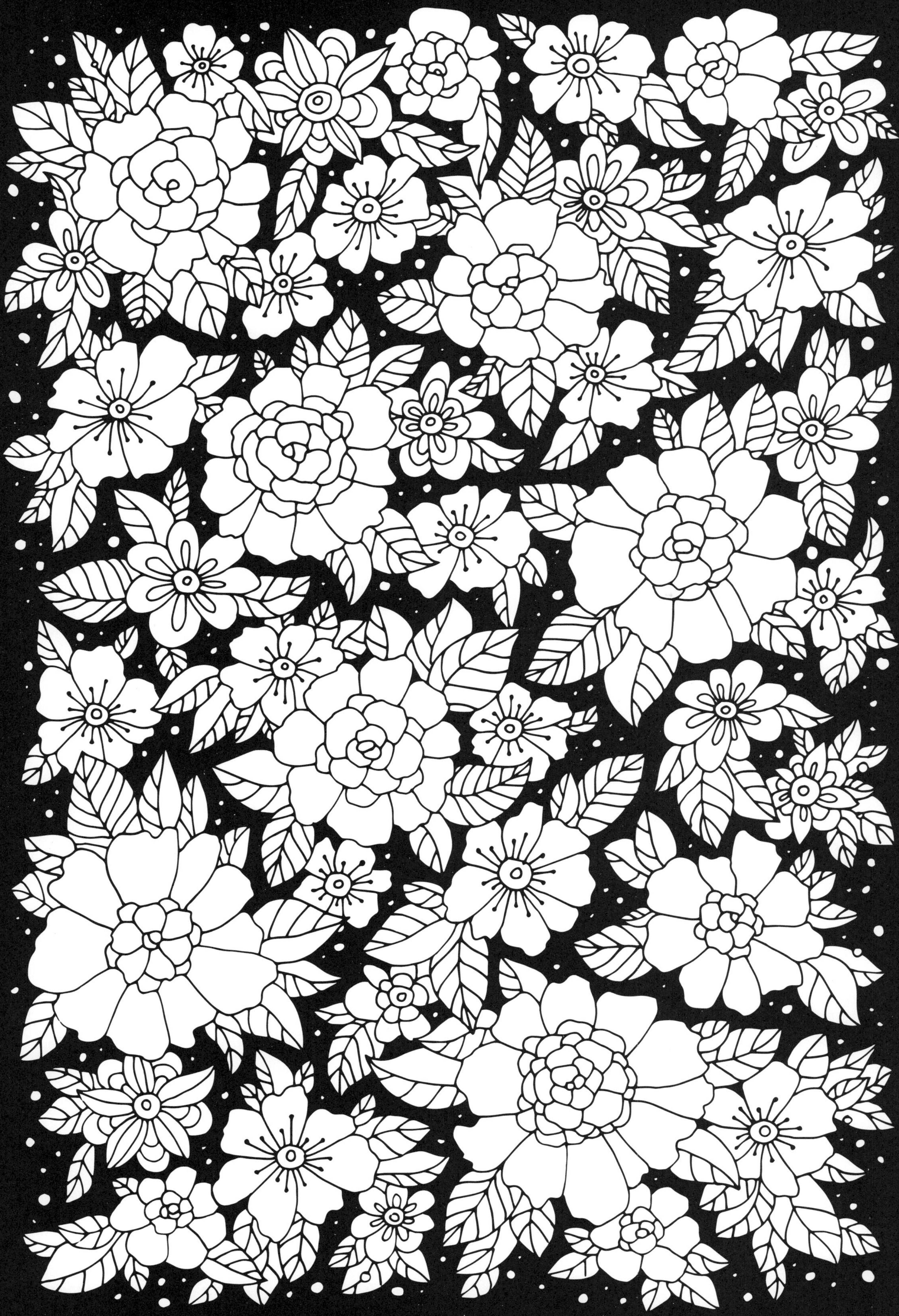

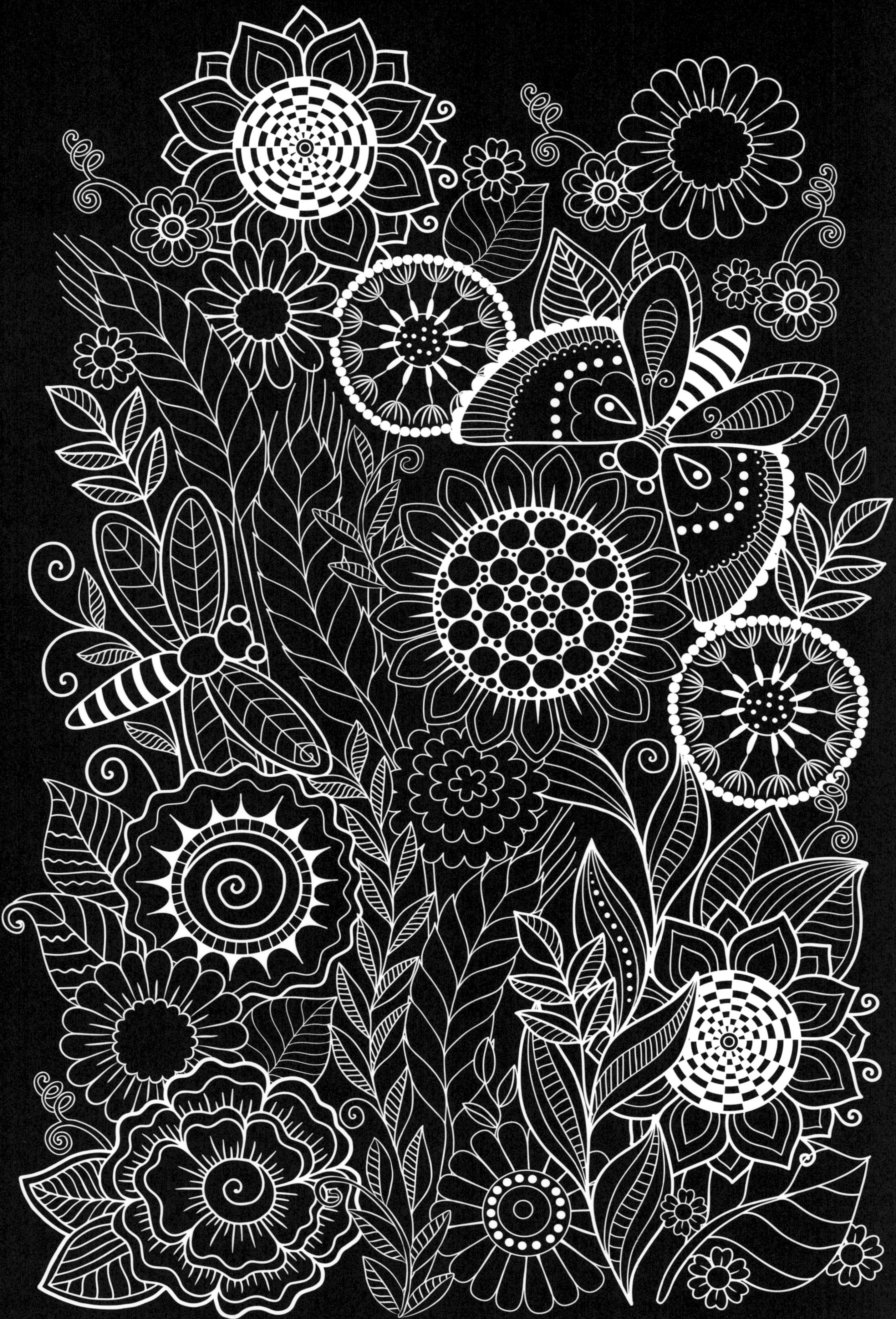

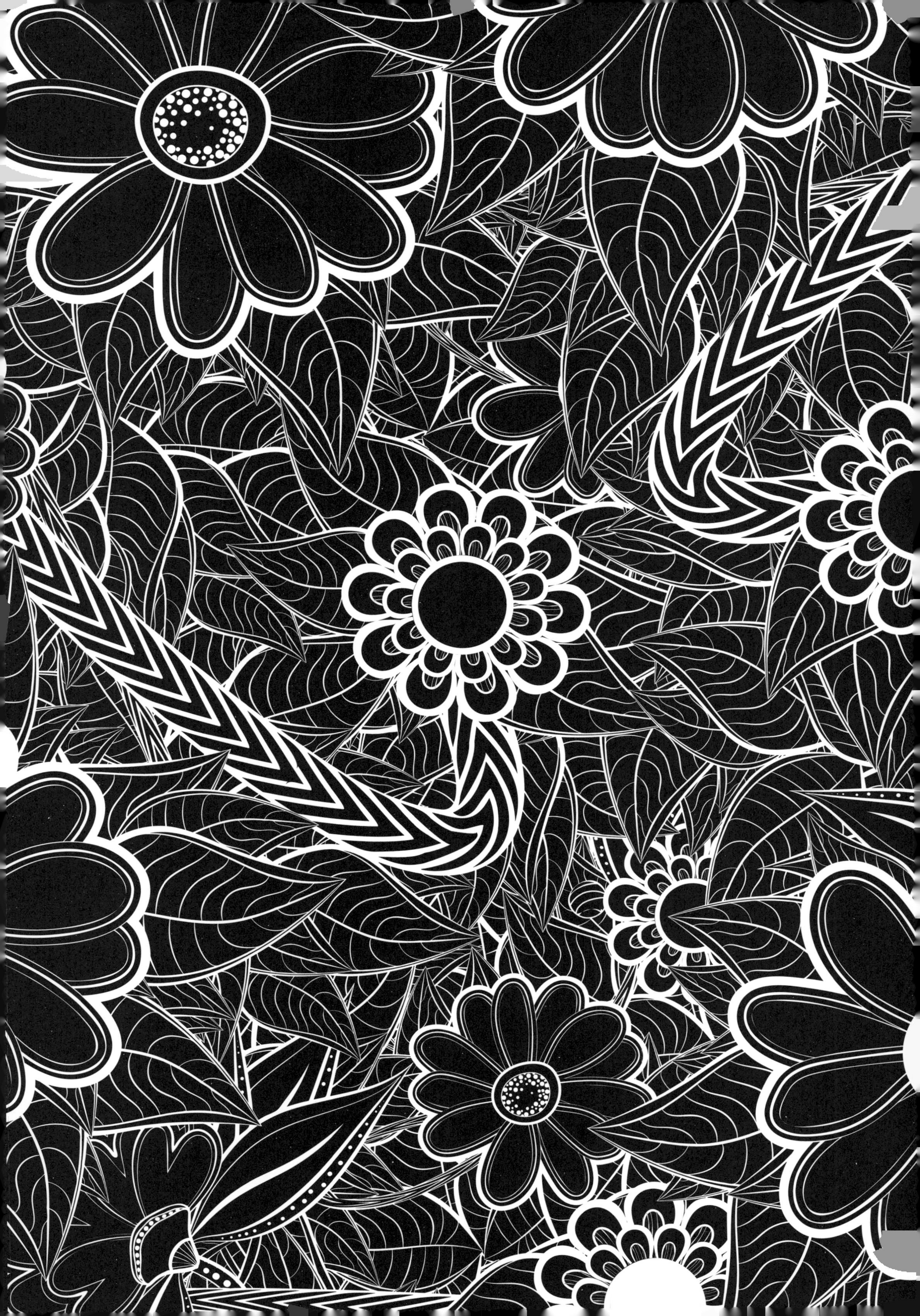

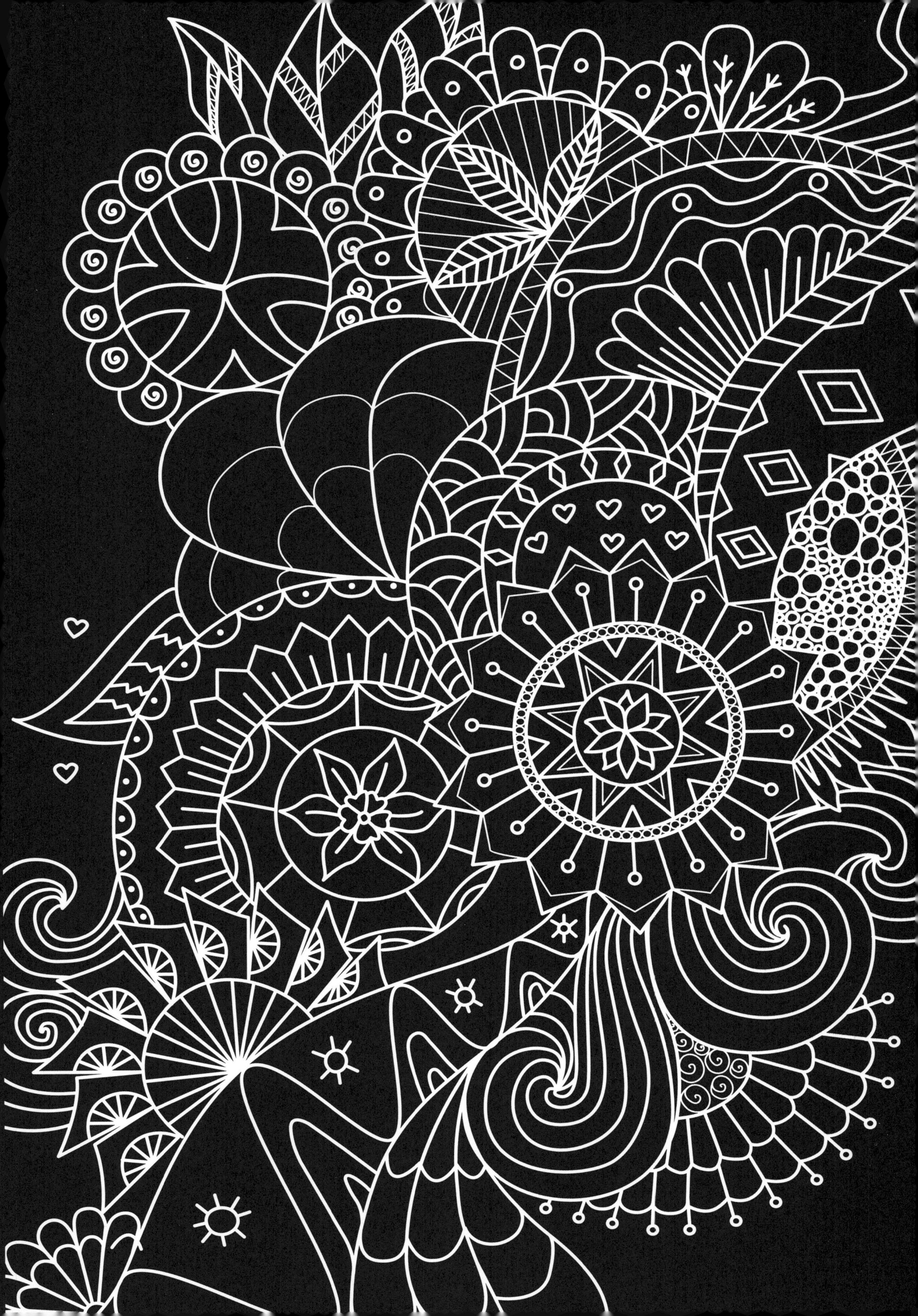

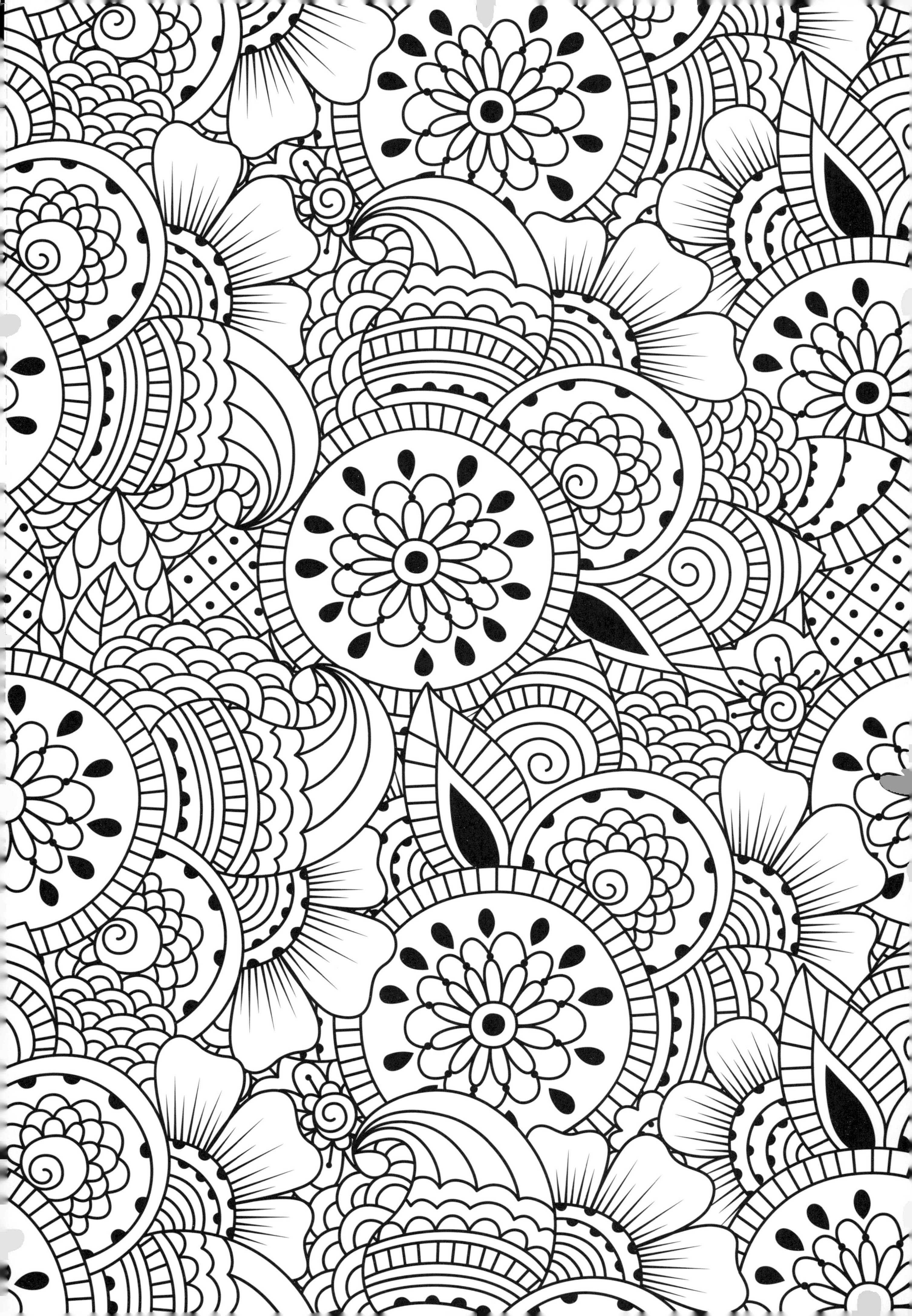

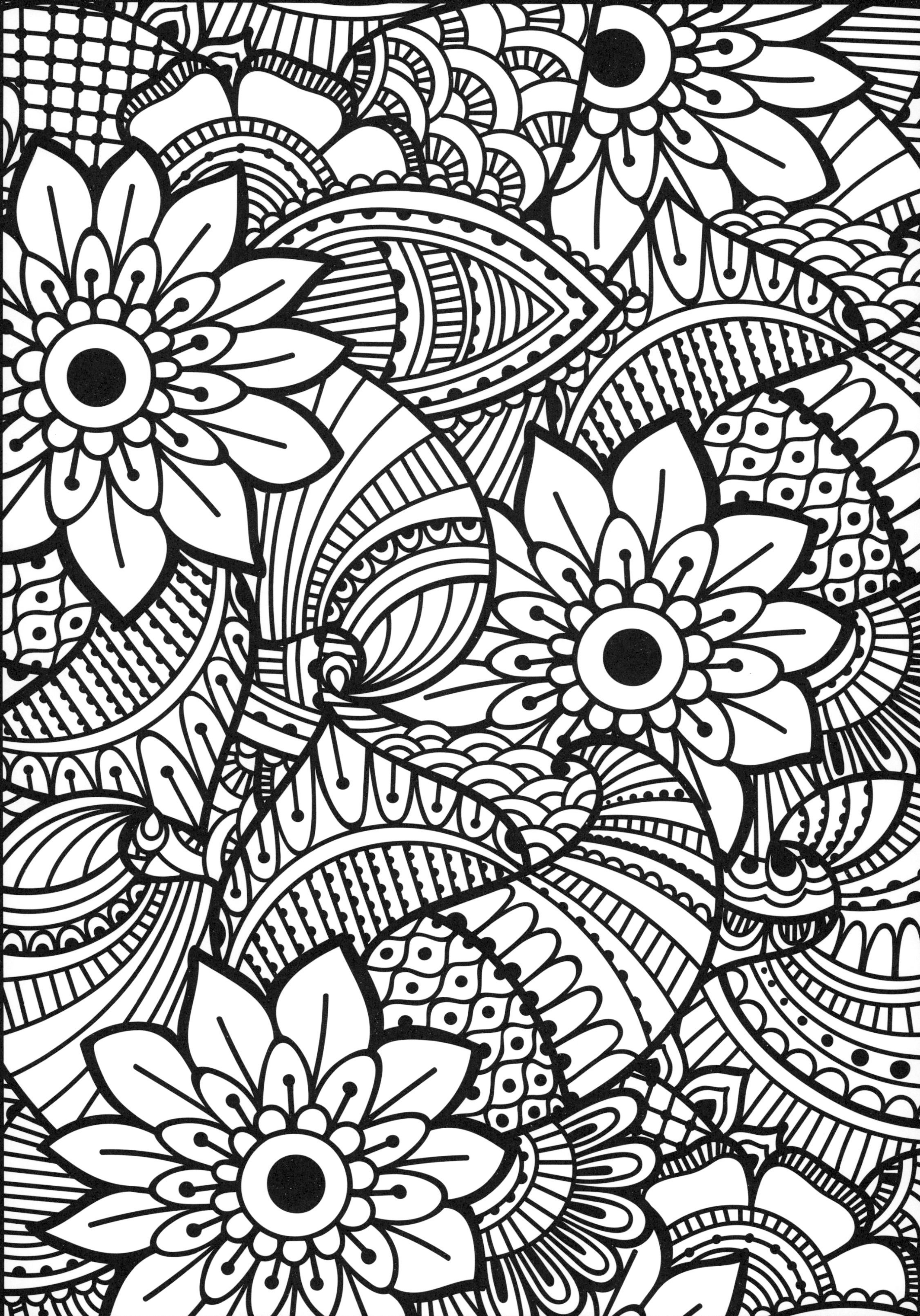

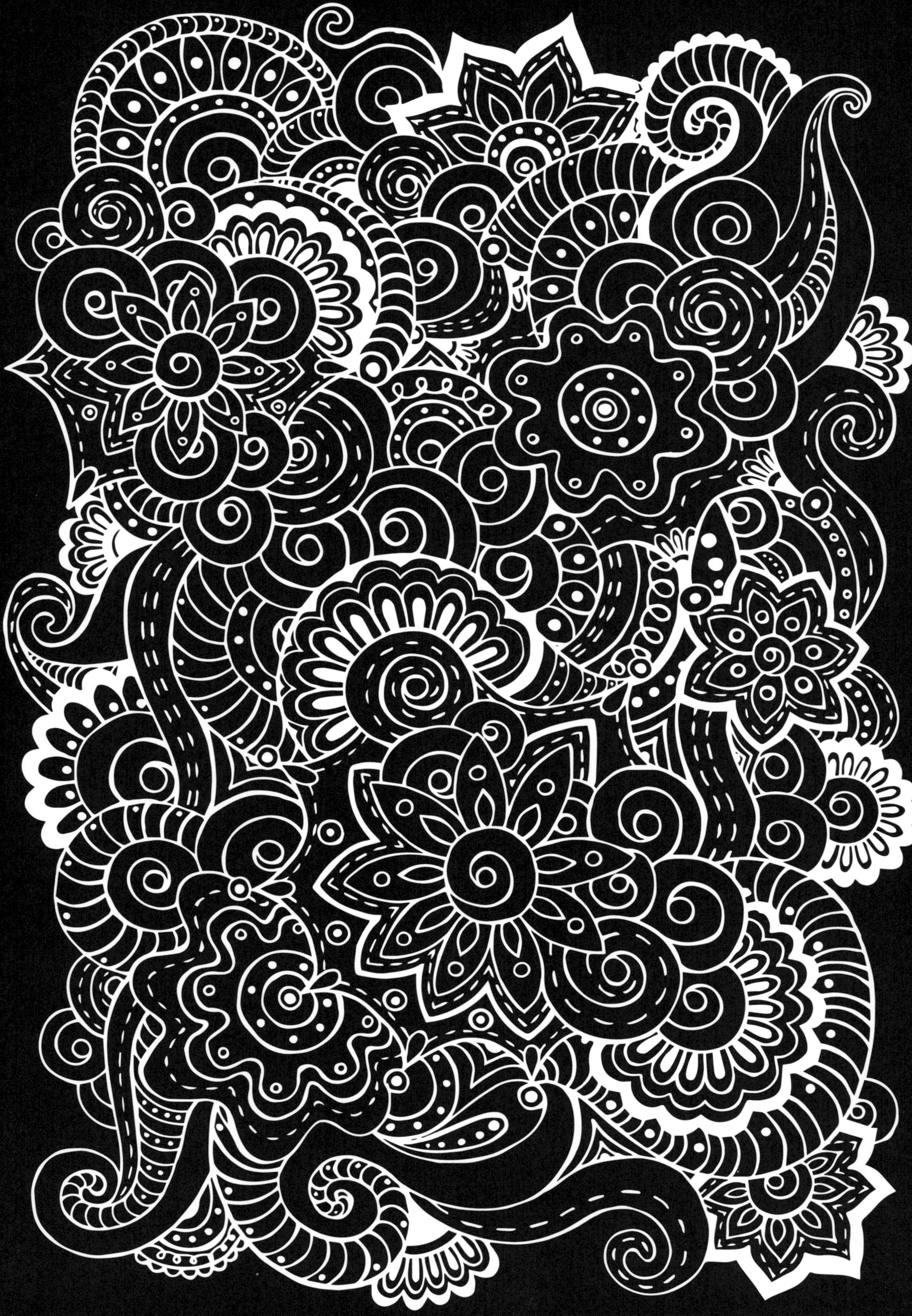

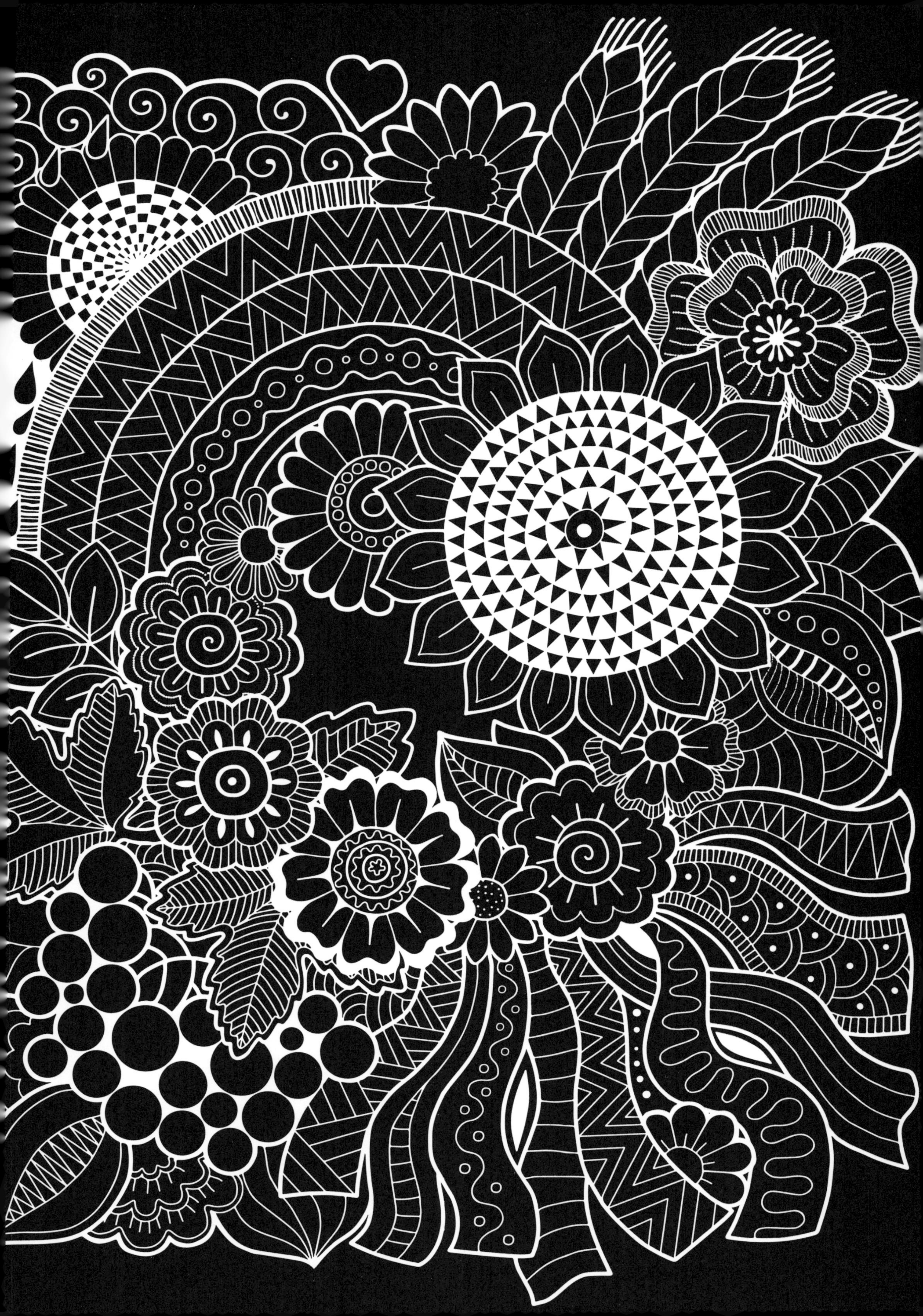

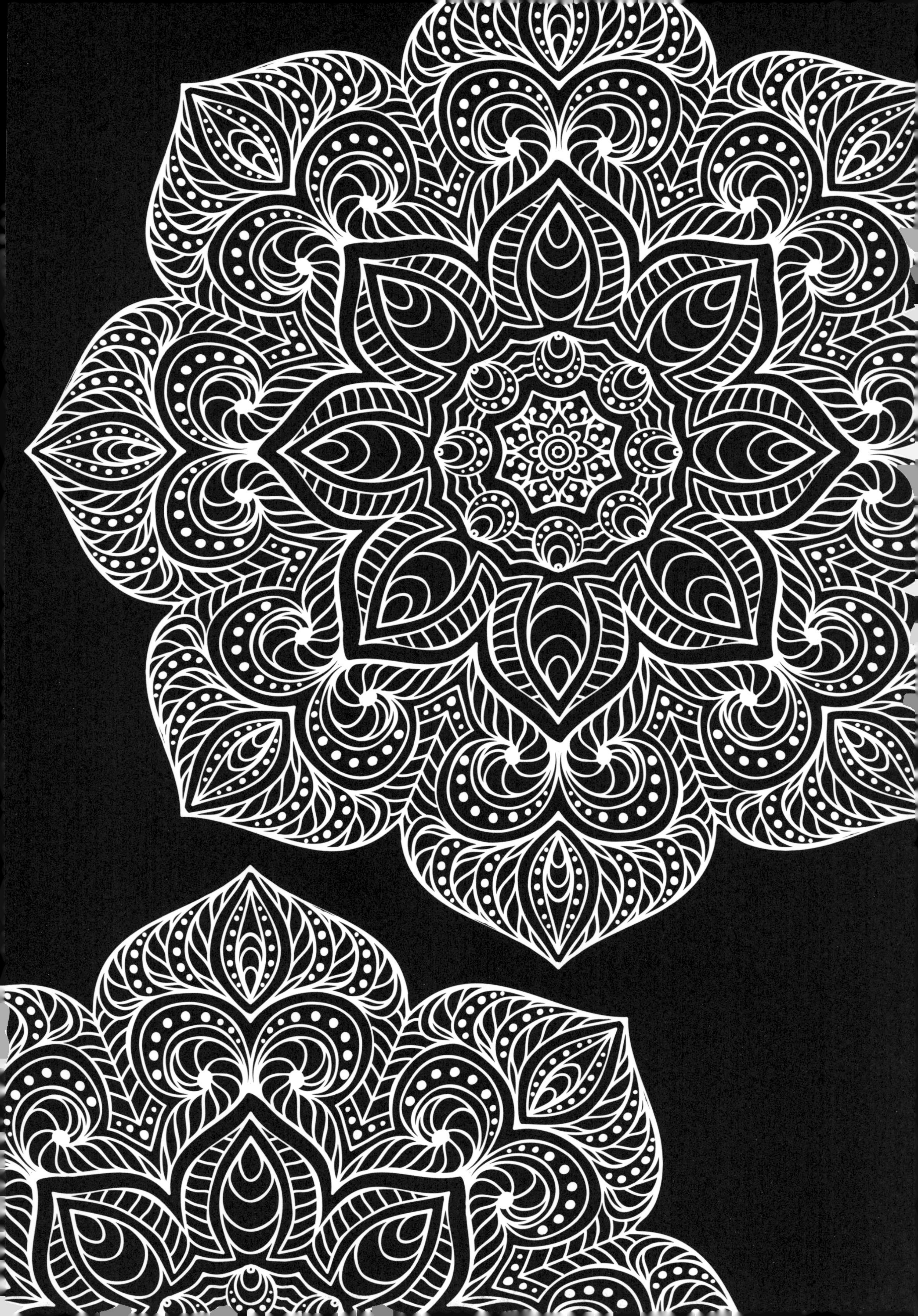

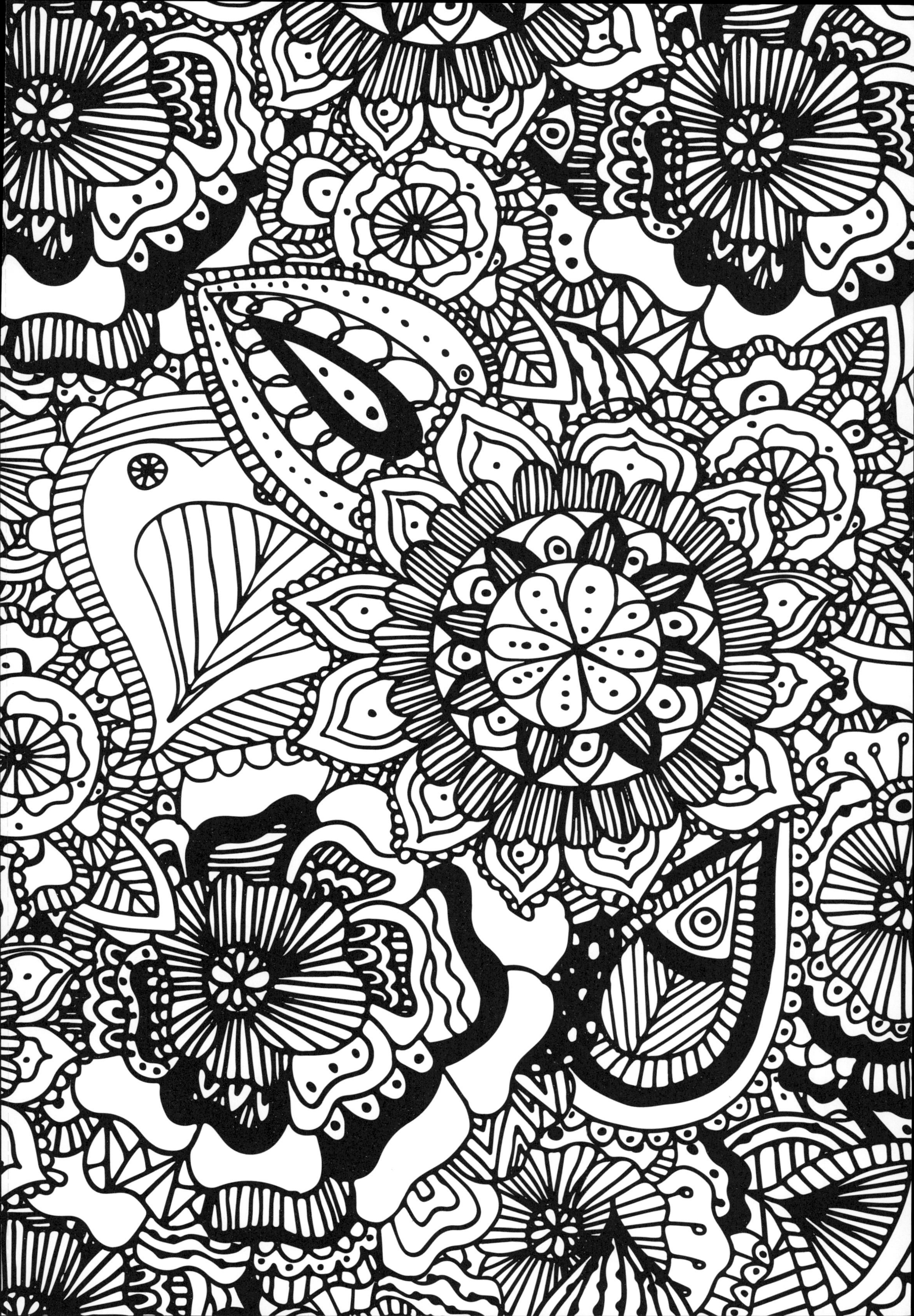

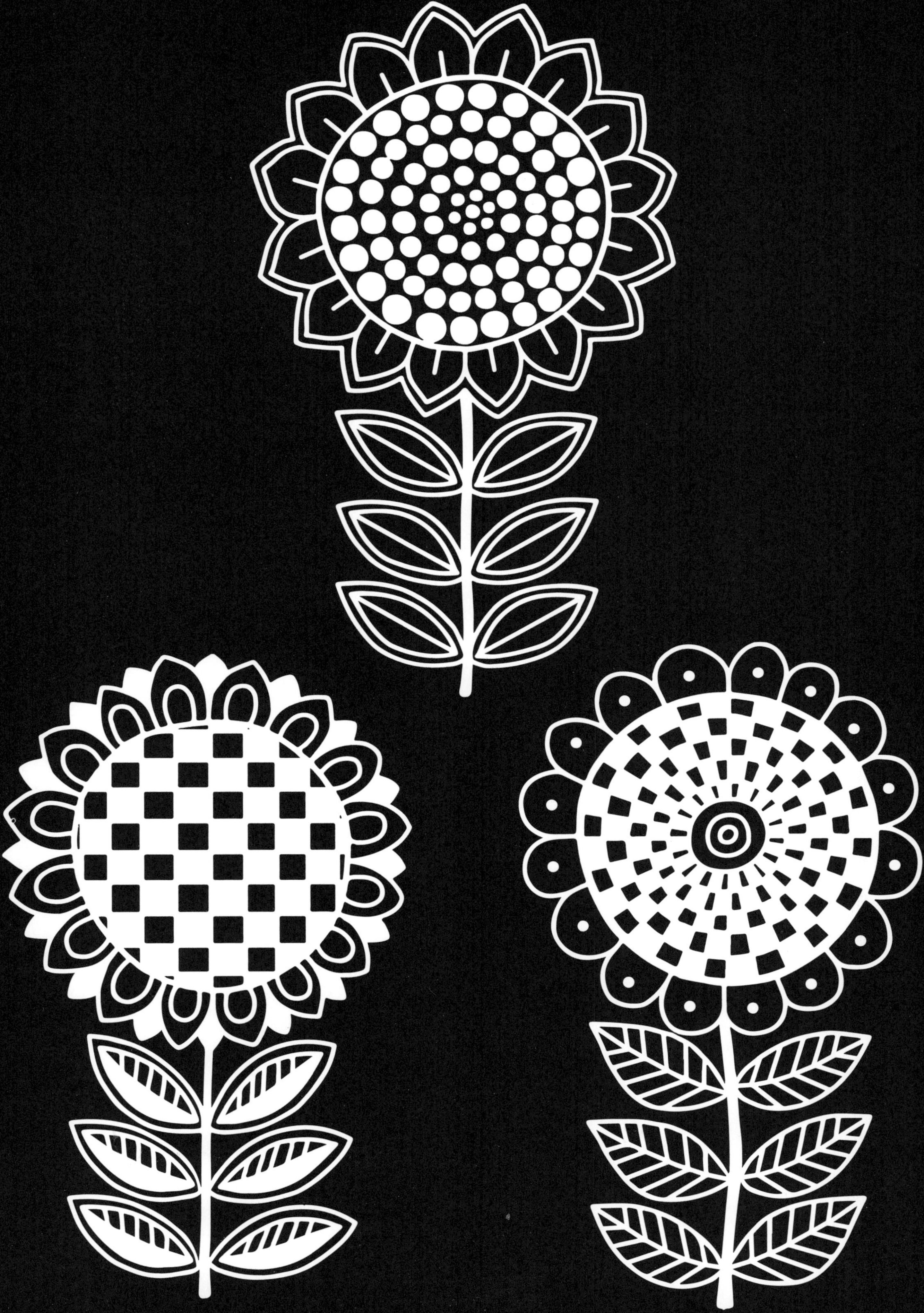

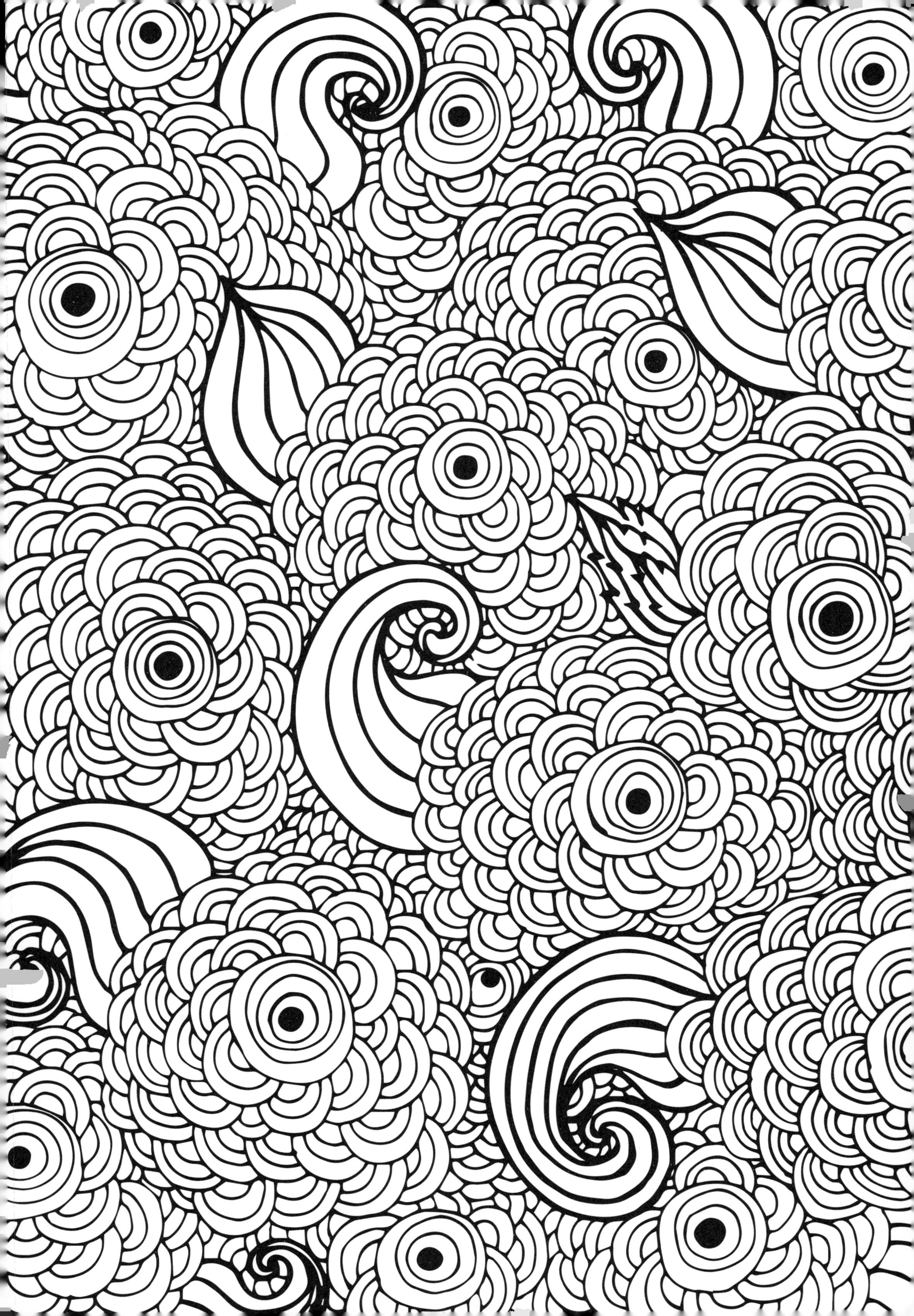

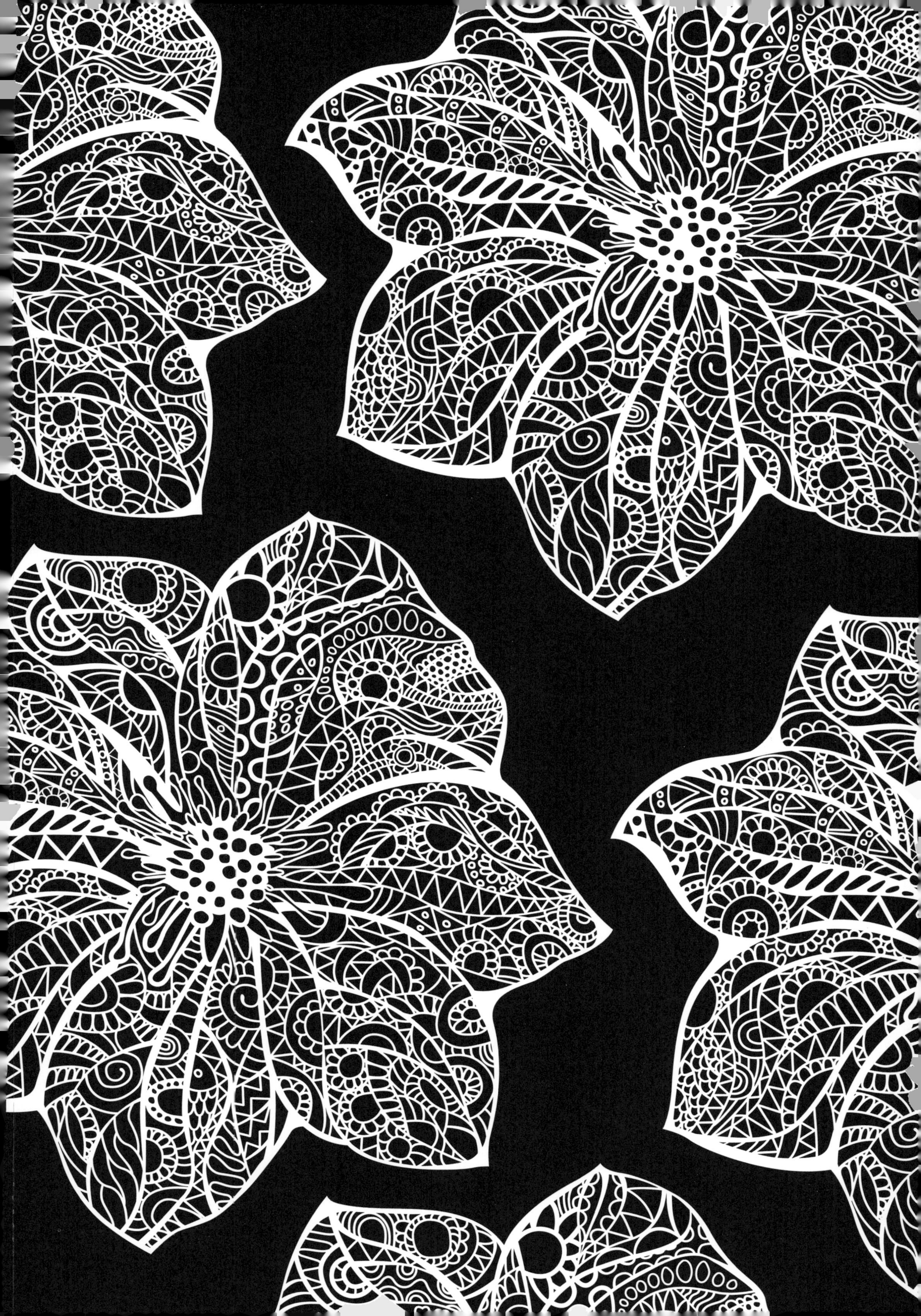